DICTATORSHIP

DICTATORSHIP

ODYSSEYS

JENNIFER FANDEL

CREATIVE EDUCATION · CREATIVE PAPERBACKS

Published by Creative Education and Creative Paperbacks
P.O. Box 227, Mankato, Minnesota 56002
Creative Education and Creative Paperbacks are imprints of
The Creative Company
www.thecreativecompany.us

Book design by Blue Design (www.bluedes.com)
Art direction by Rita Marshall
Printed in China

Photographs by Alamy (ALIKI SAPOUNTZI/aliki image library, Mary Evans
Picture Library, Jeremy Nicholl, George Philipas, Popperfoto, Homer Sykes),
Corbis (Yannis Kontos), Getty Images (AFP, Hulton Archive, Matt Moyer,
Popperfoto, Time Life Pictures, Roger Viollet)

Library of Congress Cataloging-in-Publication Data
Fandel, Jennifer.
Dictatorship / Jennifer Fandel.
p. cm. — (Odysseys in government)
Includes bibliographical references and index.
Summary: An examination of the dictatorial form of government, including
its basic ideologies and structure, its best-known leaders throughout history,
and countries affected by its system of rule.

ISBN 978-1-60818-725-6 (hardcover)
ISBN 978-1-62832-321-4 (pbk)
ISBN 978-1-56660-760-5 (eBook)
1. Dictatorship. 2. Dictators.

JC495.F36 2016
321.9—dc23   2015048535

CCSS: RI.8.1, 2, 3, 4; RI.9-10.1, 2, 3, 4; RI.11-12.1, 2, 3, 4; RH.6-8.1, 4, 5, 7;
RH.9-10.1, 3, 4

First Edition HC 9 8 7 6 5 4 3 2 1
First Edition PBK 9 8 7 6 5 4 3 2 1

CONTENTS

Government, like the brain in a body, is the control center of a country. It collects information and dispatches orders to keep all parts of the country running smoothly.

Just as a brain cannot act alone, but requires, among other things, the nerves that sense changes throughout the body and tell the brain how to act, the government cannot act alone. It needs citizens

OPPOSITE:

to govern and requires the assistance of many people to carry out its orders. Likewise, the brain's ultimate purpose is to keep the body safe and working properly, just as most governments work to ensure the safety and order of their countries.

However, in the government system known as dictatorship, the brain has total control and disregards information coming from the rest of the body. Complete power of a country rests in the hands of one leader, the dictator, who rules with no restrictions—in law or **constitution**—on his power. Because power is in the hands of one person, that person's personality and ideas affect the government as a whole.

Dictatorships come in many forms, with each form emphasizing different aspects of the dictator's power. In today's use, the word "dictator" is typically negative.

However, when the Roman government established the first dictatorships around 300 B.C., the word was positive. The Romans developed dictatorships to help restore order in the Roman **republic**, and they limited the length and strength of the dictator's rule. Since that time, dictatorship has evolved into a government system in which power is seldom given up once a leader has obtained it.

Dictatorships today can be categorized as power-seeking, **ideological**, or a combination of the two. The military dictatorship is an example of a power-seeking dictatorship. In most situations, military dictators try to stay in power simply to maintain their position in the government and society. They don't intend to change things in their country. They simply hold on to their position, enjoying the power, status, and wealth it entails.

Ideological dictatorships are more common. In order

to appeal to the citizens of a country, a dictator has to make clear why his new **regime** is worthy of support. Dictators usually focus on a problem area in government or society, providing an ideology as a "fix" for that problem. For example, dictators might focus on the **economy**, the country's position in the world, or politics. After naming a problem, dictators claim that an ideology, such as **nationalism** or **communism**, will either save the country or harm it.

The third scenario, the coupling of power and ideology, gives the dictator both power and a reason to use that power. Usually, dictatorships in developed nations rely on ideology and couple it with military or police power. The Soviet Union built its dictatorship around communism. In Germany, Adolf Hitler (1889–1945) structured his dictatorship upon his belief in a superior

Adolf Hitler, Nazi dictator of Germany

Aryan race, a term he used to describe white Christian people from northern Europe.

Dictators typically come to power in times of transition or upheaval. While there were dictatorships throughout Europe less than a century ago, the majority of European countries stabilized, the dictatorships dissolved, and the countries created republics or **democracies**. Dictators still hold power in several countries throughout Asia, Africa, and Central America, however.

Dictatorships can take control of a country in a

number of ways. In a military dictatorship, the military seizes control of the government, overthrowing the previous leaders and installing the dictator. Other dictatorial regimes come to power through revolution. By overthrowing the previous leader, the citizens give the dictator the chance to step into power. This was the case in Russia when communist leader Vladimir Lenin (1870–1924) led the Russian Revolution in 1917 to overthrow the **monarchy** and establish himself as dictator.

Some dictators go through normal government channels to take power. In many instances, dictators gain citizen support by starting or leading a political party in a time of crisis or economic difficulty, or after a civil war. Once they gain enough votes in an election, these leaders declare that they have the people's support to do whatever they deem necessary. This is how Alexander Lukashenko

Machiavelli's *The Prince*

Niccolo Machiavelli (1469–1527) was an Italian author and politician. In his book *The Prince*, he explains the best ways for a leader to obtain and keep power. From this book came the term "Machiavellian," used to describe a cunning and cruel leader.

"I say that every prince must desire to be considered merciful and not cruel. He must, however, take care not to misuse this mercifulness…. A prince, therefore, must not mind incurring the charge of cruelty for the purpose of keeping his subjects united and faithful; for, with a very few examples, he will be more merciful than those who, from excess of tenderness, allow disorders to arise, from whence spring bloodshed and rapine [robbery]; for these as a rule injure the whole community, while the executions carried out by the prince injure only individuals.

"From this arises the question whether it is better to be loved more than feared, or feared more than loved. The reply is, that one ought to be both feared and loved, but as it is difficult for the two to go together, it is much safer to be feared than loved, if one of the two has to be wanting."

(1954–) became dictator of the republic of Belarus. In 1994, Lukashenko was elected president; two years later, he had the constitution rewritten to give himself more power and restrict the power of the **parliament**.

While each dictatorship is slightly different, most are structured along similar lines. The dictator presides over the lawmaking branch of government and appoints a cabinet, or council of ministers, to help carry out his policies relating to everything from education to military funding. Also, all political parties—except the party of the dictator—are outlawed. There is a delicate balance of authority between the dictator and his party. While dictatorships are built around the rule of the dictator, he would be unable to hold his position for long without the support of the party.

The structure of a military dictatorship is slightly different from other dictatorships since the military, rather than a party, is the focus of the government. Most military dictatorships are ruled by a junta, a Spanish word meaning "conference" or "board." The military's top leadership forms the junta, and the dictator is typically appointed by this group. The leader in a military dictatorship isn't always a member of the military; sometimes civilian dictators carry out the policies of the military regime. A civilian dictator may help give the appearance of a government separate from the military.

Some dictatorships try to extend their power beyond the typical limits of government, such as the economy, laws, and social services. They want control of all aspects of their citizens' lives, including their attitudes and beliefs. These dictatorships are known as totalitarian, a term used by Italian dictator Benito Mussolini (1883–1945) in the 1920s. In a totalitarian government, there is no separation between the government and society. The goal of this type of dictatorship is to create a "perfect" society out of the existing society. Under this system, citizens are expected to serve and respect the government as the ultimate authority in their lives, similar to the relationship between a parent and a young child.

In totalitarian dictatorships, cults of personality are common. Governments are characterized as cults of personality when their main mission—above all other aspects of government—is to honor the dictator. The dictator and his close associates build up his image

Poster of former Iraqi dictatorial president Saddam Hussein

so that he appears godlike: all-powerful, all-knowing, and infallible. The government wants people to believe that the country would fall apart if not for the work of the dictator.

Totalitarian dictators, in their quest for power over their citizens, typically use **propaganda** to spread the larger-than-life personality they have created for themselves. In order to bring this personality to the forefront of people's consciousness, dictators may have their images prominently displayed throughout the country on billboards, in television broadcasts, and within public buildings. In Germany in the 1930s, for example, a picture of Hitler was required in every public building. More recently, before the overthrow of Iraqi dictator Saddam Hussein (1937–2006) in 2003, each news broadcast in the country began with a reference to the dictator's good deeds. This type of propaganda is meant to glorify the dictator and fill citizens with emotion, whether it be fear or firm allegiance to the dictator.

After dictators have used propaganda to spread their message, they usually use it to hold on to their power. Dictators often claim that they are saving the country from a crisis, and it's crucial that they make citizens believe this, whether or not it is true. Even after a crisis subsides, the dictatorship may invent new crises to keep the public in a state of insecurity or fear. By maintaining these heightened feelings, the dictator has an easier time staying in control.

Power, ultimately, is the most important concern in a dictatorship. Typically, the military and police work hand-in-hand with the dictator and his government. Some dictatorships are referred to as police states because of their brutality and use of intimidation techniques. In this type of government, secret police constantly gather information on citizens, which helps intensify fear of the dictator. The information they gather is interpreted—sometimes incorrectly—by the dictator and his leadership. Additionally, people are arrested, terrorized, and sometimes killed randomly. No one knows if—or when—the government might come for them.

In the Dictator's Hands

Throughout history, citizens often have initially supported dictatorships, lured into believing dictators' promises of security and stability. In time, however, citizens become disillusioned with dictatorships. Since the actions of a dictator are without consequences, he may break moral and ethical standards, as well as laws, while in power. These actions often have lasting effects on the people who live under them.

OPPOSITE:

Dictatorships, first and foremost, don't allow political **dissent**. The dictator is the law; he does what he wants without fear of retaliation or rebellion by the people. Under such a system, the dictator expects all citizens to be loyal members of his party. Anyone who tries to organize another party or speaks out against the government is typically imprisoned or exiled for an indefinite period of time. Under the rule of extremely ruthless dictators, those committing such actions against the government are often executed. For example, Joseph Stalin (1879–1953), the communist dictator of the Soviet Union from 1929 to 1953, personally composed lists of dissidents he wanted the secret police to kill. He also ordered many thousands of dissidents sent to hard labor camps in Siberia.

In order to maintain control, dictators also work to ensure that their people hear only what the government

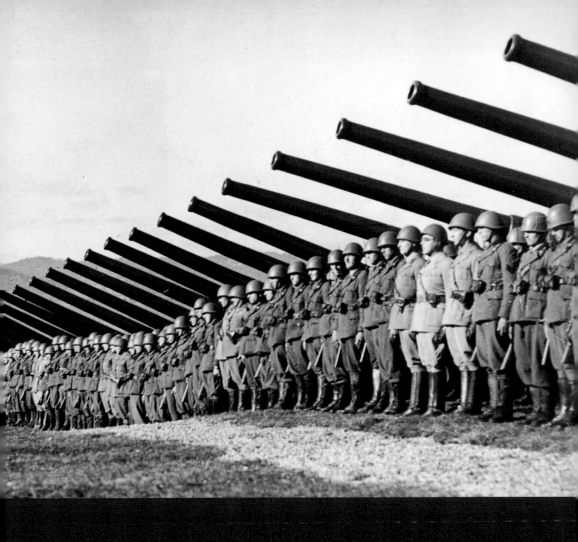

During the last century, military dictatorships sprang to life around the globe, most commonly in Latin America, Africa, and the Middle East. In these areas of the globe, governments are often not as well organized and funded as the military. A strong military can often overpower a weak government.

Since the 1990s, however, military dictatorships have become less common. One of the main reasons for this change is the fall of communism in the Soviet Union and Eastern Europe. Before the 1990s, militaries could claim that they were taking power to save their government from communism. They often could also gain the support of other countries that were against communism. Today, fighting communism is no longer a valid excuse for the establishment of a dictatorship.

Another possible reason for the decline of military dictatorships may be that most countries involved in international relations look down upon this form of government. Foreign leaders often provide incentives, such as better trade relations or foreign investment, to encourage dictators to give up their quest for power and allow citizens to have a voice in their government.

СТВУЮТ СОВЕТСКИЕ ЛЕТЧИКИ-ГО

wants them to hear. Thus, freedom of the press is nonexistent under dictatorships. In fact, many media sources, such as newspaper and publishing industries, as well as radio and television broadcasting, are run or controlled by the government. Opposing views are not reported. **Censorship** of "unacceptable" political or social content that comes from outside of the country is another common way for dictatorships to take away the freedom of the press. Satellite dishes are banned, foreign broadcasts are scrambled, and printed materials are confiscated. By limiting freedom of the press, dictators hope to lead their citizens to believe that they are protecting them from the terrors of the world outside their country.

Overall, dictators see no difference between their citizens' public and private lives. In fact, under most dictatorships, the right to privacy does not exist. In the

not stand alone as individuals; the dictator expects them to become supporting members of the community he has set up. Their personal beliefs—including their religion, culture, and sexual orientation—need to be suppressed, hidden, or even officially changed to satisfy the government.

In many dictatorships, one way of life is sanctioned, or approved, as correct. The government may declare that one **ethnic** group or religion is to be valued, while other ethnic groups or religions should be abolished. Under such regimes, people of unsanctioned groups may be discriminated against or even killed. Such actions were seen during World War II, when German Nazis (National **Socialists**) under Adolf Hitler's leadership killed the Jewish people living in their country and throughout Europe. The Nazis sent Jewish people to concentration camps where they were worked to death or sent to their

Most nations in the world obey international laws of warfare relating to the treatment of civilians, care of the sick and wounded, and the types of weapons that can be used. Actions such as   and rape are against the rules of war. Despite these rules, executions, abuse, and the use of terror and force are commonplace under dictatorships, as the dictator and his supporters do whatever is necessary to retain their power over others.

Since World War II, war criminals have been tried in court and punished for their actions, with some receiving the death penalty. In 2002, international trials in the Netherlands began for Serbia's former president, Slobodan Milosevic (1941–2006). He was accused of ordering genocides and rapes throughout the former Yugoslavia. He died before the trials ended.

In 2005, Saddam Hussein was brought to trial for his role in genocides committed in Iraq; he was sentenced to death and was hanged in December 2006. In setting up a democracy, the people of Iraq chose to put Hussein on trial in his own country. They believed their legal system would be able to provide Hussein a fair and just trial.

death in gas chambers. Genocides are still common oc-
currences under dictatorships today.

The freedom to worship is also forbid-
den in many dictatorships. Under
some dictatorships, public worship
has been banned, and religious statues, places of worship,
and relics have been destroyed. In Iraq, for example, Saddam Hussein's government destroyed many mosques and
holy sites sacred to the Shia people, a minority Muslim
group. Dictators often think that the destruction of these
symbols will diminish the credibility of the religion and

erase thoughts of it from the public's mind. In many cases, the dictator believes that his people should worship only himself and his government.

In some dictatorships, worship isn't against the law, although the government specifies what citizens must believe. Religions may be government-sanctioned, with only certain types of worship receiving approval. Those who worship outside of these government rules can be punished for dissent. The Chinese government, for example, approves only five religions: Catholicism, Protestantism, Buddhism, Taoism, and Islam. In 1999, China's communist dictatorship made the Falun Gong spiritual movement illegal. Leaders of the movement were arrested, and some members were put into mental hospitals.

While the ethnicity, culture, or religion of a citizen is often under scrutiny in a dictatorship, a citizen's work may also be examined to make sure that it meets the values or goals of the dictatorship. The work of scholars, scientists, and artists may be censored, and those whose works invite controversy may be exiled or detained. Similarly, those with expertise in certain subjects may be ordered to support efforts by the government. The government may demand that scientists work on weapons programs. Scholars may be told to rewrite aspects of history, and artists may be required to glorify their leader in their work.

Additionally, because the dictator makes and enforces the laws, citizens have no fair legal channels at their disposal. Even though most dictatorial governments have judicial systems, these usually are corrupt and weighted in favor of those with wealth or affiliation with the government. In the case of the western African nation of Cameroon, the courts are under the power of dictatorial president Paul Biya (1933–). Because judges are appointed and dismissed by Biya, they usually uphold his rules—even those that are unfair—in order to keep their positions.

While many countries regard voting as a right of citizens, this is typically not the case in a dictatorship. However, elections are occasionally conducted to give the appearance of a democratically run country. These elections are usually a sham, as voters are given the choice to vote only for the dictator and are often forced to vote. This was true in 1995, when Saddam Hussein—the only candidate listed on the ballot—won 99.96 percent of the vote in Iraq. Dictators organize such elections and demand participation in order to convince the world that there is **unanimous** citizen support for their government.

The general balance of power and wealth within a

dictatorial government is less than ideal for most of its citizens. Typically, those who are associated with the government and its political party hold the majority of the wealth and power in the country. Those who are faithful party members are often given benefits that others may not have access to, such as the freedom to travel abroad or send their children to good schools.

I n a dictatorship, money equals power. Wealthy supporters of the government often use bribes to get what they want. If a desired product is illegal or hard to obtain, they simply pay off government officials or the police to get it for them on the black market, which offers goods from fresh meat and vegetables to alcohol and cigarettes. Black market items may even include banned music and books.

Overall, the lack of rights under dictatorships keeps citizens in a state of weakness and fear, which ultimately helps the dictator maintain his power. British writer George Orwell (1903–50) addressed this state of fear in his novel *1984*. In the fictional dictatorship that he describes, posters reading "Big Brother is watching you" hang everywhere. No one is sure whom to trust, as they are certain that the government—their "Big Brother"—is watching their every move.

When the first dictatorships rose
to power, they were intended to
provide security for citizens—and
whole countries—in times of crisis or
difficulty. In time, dictators realized
that citizens would initially support a
dictatorship if they believed it would
make their country more stable and
secure. When faced with chaos,
especially during wartime, many
citizens look upon a strict, orderly

OPPOSITE:

government with favor. For many, it seems to be a way of moving forward and leaving the chaos behind. Such was the case for Germany, which suffered a major economic **depression** with massive unemployment after World War I. Adolf Hitler and his Nazi Party won support by promising greater stability through large public works programs to put Germans back to work.

The desire for security is still one of the most common reasons dictatorships are able to come to power today. People are often willing to give up some liberties if they feel the government will take care of them. With other dictatorships, a goal or mission unifies people. In many dictatorships, the leadership unites people around the idea of a "golden age" in the country's history and builds on people's national pride. These golden ages that dictators speak of typically never existed. They are myths that people want to believe in and are used to encourage citizens to work toward impossible goals and ignore the ever-tightening control of the dictator.

The use of national pride to unify a country also usually excludes some members of society. When citizens remember the golden ages of their country's history, they remember a time before many of the problems of the present time existed. When they search for the causes of the problems, they often focus on different ethnic groups in the country, believing that these groups brought the problems into the country with them. This was another of Hitler's tactics: he gave impassioned speeches about the glories of Germany in an imagined time before the Jews moved there and thus blamed Jews for all of Germany's troubles.

Although dictatorships tend to be riddled with problems, some hold that this government system saves

Former dictator Adolf Hitler (center) at a Nazi rally in 1934

citizens from the worries of everyday life. In totalitarian governments, especially, all aspects of a person's life are dictated by the government. People are told how to believe, how to act, and how to serve the government. In return, the government promises to supply all of their needs. The communist dictatorship in the Soviet Union promoted itself as saving people from the worries of finding jobs and feeding their families. If citizens did everything the government required, the government claimed that their lives would be freed from practical concerns. This claim, however, never came true.

Like people in the Soviet Union, most citizens under dictatorships find that total obedience to the government, rather than providing all of their necessities, represses many of their human needs and takes away their **human rights**. Citizens feel stripped of their identities, with few, if any, choices in life. Even the simplest pleasures—enjoying a piece of music or making a favorite meal, for instance—may be beyond their control.

Additionally, bad decisions made by the dictator often eventually harm citizens, leaving them in a state of vulnerability. Some bad decisions have left countries in economic shambles, while others have created a malnourished or starving populace. Dictators often try to hide the truth about the effects of their bad decisions from the people they rule. In Italy, Mussolini often

London protest against Greek dictatorship, 1967

made grand speeches about the successes of the Italian army during World War II. Italian citizens believed his claims, and bans on outside media made it impossible for citizens to know that the army was losing battles—until they found themselves on the losing side of the war.

In time, most people tire of surrendering their freedoms to a dictator and begin to question his true intentions. They begin to see that the power structure clearly favors the dictator, as this type of government benefits government leaders above anyone else. All power truly is in the dictators' hands. They do not have to get any approval for their ideas or policies, as long as they are supported by their party. Their agenda—as well as their personal gain—is what's most important.

This power imbalance is explained by famous Russian nuclear physicist Andrei Sakharov (1921–89), who became a leading spokesperson for human rights in the 1970s. He said, "The party apparatus of government and the highest, most successful layers of the intelligentsia [well-educated class] cling tenaciously to their open and secret privileges and are profoundly indifferent to the infringement of human rights, the interest of progress, security, and the future of mankind." While many would state that those at the top layers of government and society within dictatorships *don't* care about the citizens they govern, some might argue that they *can't* care. They are too busy protecting their own interests, and caring would reveal a weakness—possibly even a connection to the people they are supposed to serve.

Wealth is one of the biggest privileges that a dictator and his government colleagues enjoy. While citizens governed by a dictator may live in poverty, those affiliated with the government often hoard the country's wealth. In Iraq, for example, the "oil for food" program run by the United Nations allowed humanitarian food supplies to come into the country in exchange for the country's oil. The government, however, gave many of the supplies to the military and the country's elite. Additionally, Saddam Hussein had great palaces built for himself, decked with marble and gold.

Despite the wealth and power they enjoy while in office, most dictators find that they have to work constantly to maintain control. They must continually appeal to the emotions of their citizens, keeping them in a state of obedience, fear, or nationalistic pride. Such was the situation during the Spanish Civil War (1936–39) when one of dictator Francisco Franco's (1892–1975) generals, Emilio Mola (1887–1937), said: "It is necessary to spread an atmosphere of terror. We have to create an impression of mastery." Franco and his troops committed atrocious acts, including massive bombings of the small Spanish town of Guernica, to bring the Spanish people under their control.

If a dictator lets his power slip even slightly, people may question his authority or begin planning ways to overthrow him. Thus, the dictator must maintain a strong power structure, for without the help of the police or military, a dictator is unable to forward his agenda. When the power structure fails, the dictator rapidly loses control of the country. That is why dictatorships usually come to bitter ends. Afterwards, dictators, government officials, the military, and the police have often found themselves accused of crimes against humanity, and many of them have been sentenced for the killings and

The western African nation of Cameroon declared itself a republic in 1972. The government's actions, however, indicate that it remains a dictatorship. While the country began allowing multiple political parties and regular elections in 1990, recent elections have been marked by fraud. In the 1997 presidential election, for example, there were many irregularities in the voting process and results, leading domestic and international observers to question the fairness and accuracy of the election.

The government of Cameroon also limits freedom of the press. All radio and television broadcasts are controlled by the government, and satellite broadcasts from other countries are severely restricted. Additionally, journalists are subjected to harassment and death threats from the government if they print anything that discredits those who rule the country.

Despite these problems, domestic and international human rights organizations have the freedom to conduct investigations and publish their findings. The government occasionally makes their jobs more difficult, however, by blocking access to prisoners or refusing to share information. Nonetheless, this one freedom gives people hope that Cameroon may soon give in to outside pressure to improve its human rights situation, which might, in turn, help the country eventually live up to its status as a republic.

torture that took place under their rule.

Overall, world leaders are wary of the leadership of dictators. In very few circumstances are they seen in a good light. However, democratic governments have occasionally supported dictators in order to overthrow a previous ruler. This was quite common in the 1970s and '80s when the United States hoped to get rid of communist governments around the world. In 1973, the

Spanish dictator Francisco Franco

U.S. helped organize a military coup against Salvador Allende (1908–73), the socialist president of Chile, and had him replaced with dictator Augusto Pinochet (1915–2006).

Even in cases of supported dictatorships, the world community usually discovers that the dictatorship spirals out of control. While it may appear to be a solution at the time, it most often creates more problems than good. Most disturbing to the world community is the fact that it's difficult to negotiate with a dictator. Once a dictator assumes power, he is not likely to willingly give it up.

Moreover, many dictators hope to expand their regimes once they take power. In the mindset of a dictator, the world exists to be conquered. As a result, dictatorships create instability around the globe. They often breed war, poverty, and troubled international relationships. The international community often takes responsibility for the citizens living under dictatorships; food aid is supplied, and political refugees are taken in by many countries. Countries located close to the dictator may also feel the need to plan weapons programs or alliances with other countries in case the dictator ever makes threats, begins invasions, or declares war in the region.

Augusto Pinochet obtained his position as dictator of the Chilean government in 1973. His predecessor, president Salvador Allende, pushed a socialist agenda that included land reform and government takeover of industries. The perceived threat of a communist-socialist government encouraged the U.S. to help bring Allende's government down. Allende was overthrown in a bloody military coup, and Augusto Pinochet took over as president.

What no one foresaw was Pinochet's love of power. He ordered more than 2,000 political assassinations and used mass arrests to exercise power over his people. He used terror, murder, and kidnapping against anyone who did not support his regime. The thousands who were kidnapped, called "the disappeared," are believed to be dead, since most were never found. Although Pinochet stepped down as president in 1990 after losing a special election that would have allowed him to rule for eight more years, he remained a Chilean senator until 2002. Between 2000 and Pinochet's death in December 2006, there were debates between the international community and Chile over bringing the aging dictator to trial for his crimes.

Dictatorships
around the World

The first dictatorships began around
300 B.C. in ancient Rome. These
dictatorships, however, were used only
·in times of emergency, such as during
a war or civil unrest. Dictators held
their positions for only six months at a
time. The Roman government had rid
itself of its monarchy only 200 years
before and replaced this government
with a constitutional republic. From
their knowledge of that earlier time,

OPPOSITE:

the Romans believed it was wise to limit the authority of an individual in power.

In these early Roman dictatorships, dictators were not voted into power by the citizens as were other politicians in ancient Rome. However, the dictators had to be nominated by government officials and confirmed by a special committee. Other government officials, such as judges and lawmakers, were able to remain in office, but they had to answer to the dictator.

Similar to present dictatorships, the policies of the Roman dictator could not be vetoed by other government officials. He was the ultimate authority in Rome for his six-month term. In contrast to present times, however, the Roman dictator had limits on his power. He was accountable for his actions after the state of emergency, and all of his decisions were subject to the constitution and the law. He could not make or break laws as he saw fit.

While this form of dictatorship worked well, it did not last. By the second century B.C., civil wars broke out in Rome, and individuals rose to power, shaping governments based on their own desires. One of these governments was that of Julius Caesar (100–44 B.C.). Active in Roman politics, Caesar built his reputation through his military conquests. He eventually held a number of political positions, and his popularity grew after he led the Roman army in its conquest of Gaul, the Roman name for a large area of northern Europe.

Believing that he could govern the Roman Empire better than those in power, Caesar turned his army on Rome and took over the city.

In 46 B.C., Caesar made himself dictator of Rome and claimed that this position was for life. This was against the Roman constitution, and a minority of wealthy **conservatives** opposed his rule. However, Caesar had the overriding support of the rest of his citizens, to whom he promised greater opportunity and prosperity. To strengthen his rule, he **centralized** the military and government, bringing everything under his power. He cemented the support of the poor by starting building projects to put them to work. Land from his political opponents was also taken by Caesar and given to his supporters. His rule lasted only two years. His opponents organized against him and stabbed him to death.

A similar fate came to one of the most brutal dictators of the 20th century: Benito Mussolini in Italy. Mussolini's regime is known as a particular type of dictatorship called fascism. The word *fascism* comes from a symbol of ancient Roman authority called the *fasces*. This symbol, a bundle of sticks surrounding an ax, was meant to represent unified strength under a powerful leader. In fascism, the strong have rights over the weak, and the group is always put before the rights of the individual. Overall, fascists believe in using military and police strength, as well as war, to create an orderly, unified society.

Mussolini came to power in Italy between World War I and World War II, a time of economic depression and political chaos in Europe. At the time, Italy was governed by a **constitutional monarchy**. In 1921, the fascist movement won seats in Italy's parliament through popular election, and the country's king named Mussolini prime minister the next year. To gain control of the government, Mussolini encouraged his followers to begin terror campaigns. The Blackshirts, street gangs loyal to Mussolini, assassinated a parliament member. Mussolini then declared a state of emergency to establish his fascist dictatorship. He suspended Italian citizens' civil liberties, such as the freedom of speech, the right to vote, and the right to assemble. Four years later, Mussolini banned all other political parties.

Throughout his regime, which lasted from 1922 to 1943, Mussolini was able to build citizen support through his cult of personality. The dictator always appeared in a military uniform to show his strength and assert his belief in military order. Additionally, he was an excellent speaker who appeared regularly on his balcony to make

Benito Mussolini, fascist dictator of Italy

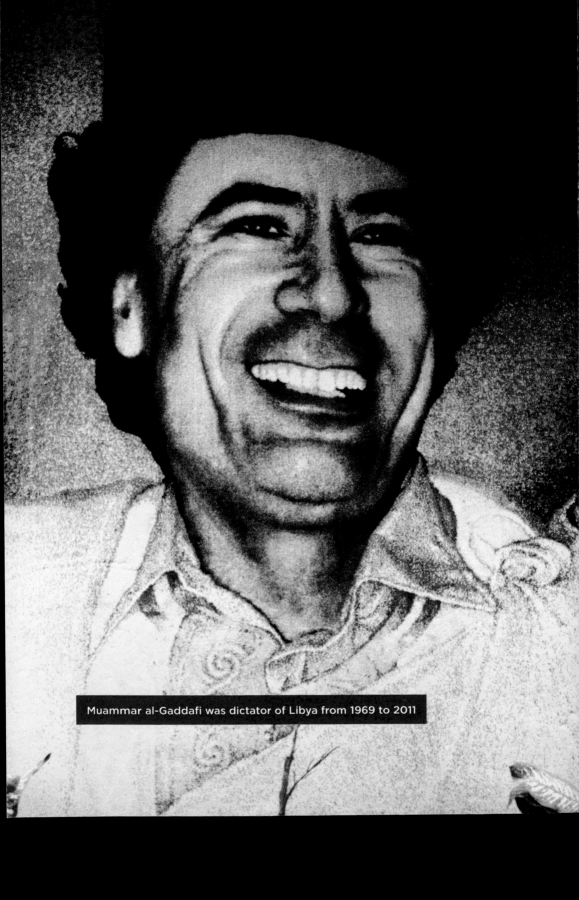

Muammar al-Gaddafi was dictator of Libya from 1969 to 2011

speeches to adoring crowds below. At a time when the Italian economy was struggling, Mussolini told people what they wanted to hear. He spoke of the government's grand projects to create new jobs, and he never missed an opportunity to tell citizens of the great new Italy they were creating by supporting his regime.

However, what Mussolini never talked about was Italy's losses in World War II, the work of the secret police, and the country's internment camps for Jews from other countries. Using the motto "Obey, Believe, Fight,"

Mussolini made it clear to Italians that they had little choice in their government. Those on the battlefields knew that Italy was not winning every battle the dictator claimed the country had won. Furthermore, citizens at home witnessed firsthand the terror campaigns used by the government. Secret police forces watched people's actions, and anyone thought to be conspiring against the government was imprisoned or killed. In addition, Mussolini tried to blame his economic problems on the Jews. Italian Jews were removed from government jobs, banned from marrying non-Jews, and forced to work in war factories after 1940. In 1945, Italy's fascist government came to an abrupt halt when Mussolini was captured by antifascists and killed by a firing squad.

n 1979, more than 30 years after the death of Mussolini, dictator Saddam Hussein came to power in Iraq after forcing his cousin, president Ahmad Hasan al-Bakr (1914–82), to resign. During the 24 years of his rule, Hussein operated a one-party police state. The Ba'ath Socialist Party was the only sanctioned party in the country, and absolute **executive** and **legislative** power rested in its hands. The police, under Hussein's orders, kept citizens in a constant state of fear through random arrests, long-term detainments, and executions.

Ultimately, Hussein hoped to control all of the Middle East. He strengthened his power by taking control of the Iraqi oil industry, funneling money into his military, and using brutality against his own people. Dissidents were detained for years in inhumane prisons, with most being subjected to torture. The execution of innocent

Juan & Eva Perón

Juan Perón (1895–1974) was the president of Argentina from 1946 to 1955 and again from 1973 to 1974. He gained prominence in the Argentinean government as an army officer who supported the fascist governments in Italy and Germany. He built a support network among the workers in his country, many of whom felt that no one but Perón cared about the situation of laborers. Once he became president, however, Perón used brutality to keep his power. He had political opponents jailed and exercised strict censorship over the press. He also controlled the education students received. He wanted to build nationalism by encouraging Argentina's children to see the country as the best in the world.

Despite his brutality, Perón was able to keep support for his presidency because of his popular wife, Eva (1919–52). She was known affectionately by the people as "Evita," a name meaning "little Eva." Formerly an actress, Evita rallied citizens behind her husband with her impassioned speeches and her support of the poor. She died of cancer in 1952 at the age of 33, and Perón's power in the government rapidly declined thereafter.

people was common practice, as was genocide, including the use of poison gas on the Kurdish people, an ethnic minority in northern Iraq.

Throughout the 1980s and 1990s, Hussein began to be seen as a threat to the Middle East as well as the rest of the world. In 1980, he led an Iraqi invasion of Iran for control of a regional waterway. Eight years later, no victor had emerged, and both countries had lost hundreds of thousands of troops. Then, in 1990, Hussein invaded and took over oil-rich Kuwait, which caused the UN to intervene. In 1991, the Iraqi army was defeated, and Hussein agreed to the terms of a UN peace treaty, which included constant monitoring of Iraq's weapons programs. In 2003, after escalating tensions between Iraq and the U.S. over its weapons programs, Hussein was overthrown by the U.S. military and international allies.

The liberation of Iraq from Hussein's dictatorial rule has revealed the instability that many countries face when emerging from dictatorships. In the days and weeks following the country's liberation, there was civil unrest. Some people looted stores, invaded homes, and stole treasures from the country's museums and Hussein's palaces. Others began campaigns to take power. While the newfound freedom after years of repression was refreshing, it was also scary. No one knew what direction the country would take. Today, the country is still struggling to get on its feet politically and economically, and violence remains an everyday part of life in the capital city of Baghdad and elsewhere in Iraq.

As long as there are periods of instability and chaos in countries, dictators will find opportunities to come to power long into the future. While the world has learned a number of lessons from dictatorships in the past, leaders are still lured by thoughts of supreme control, just as citizens are still comforted by a belief in safety and security. Dictatorships are typically not long-lasting, since people often desire freedoms once they are taken away. Nevertheless, this type of government will likely continue to emerge in countries throughout the world during times of crisis.

Timeline

300 B.C. Dictatorships begin in ancient Rome, with the dictator coming to power through special nominations by government officials.

46 B.C. Julius Caesar declares himself lifelong dictator of Rome, but is killed only two years into his rule.

A.D. 445 Attila, the king of an Asian tribe of people known as the Huns, begins his takeover of Europe and an eight-year dictatorial rule.

1533 Ivan the Terrible of Russia begins his tyrannical rule; it will last for more than 50 years.

1919 Vladimir Lenin becomes the first communist dictator of Russia. He transforms the country into the Union of Soviet Socialist Republics (USSR).

1922 Benito Mussolini becomes Italy's prime minister; he sets up a ruthlessly fascist government.

1929 Joseph Stalin begins a brutal dictatorship in the Soviet Union; he will stay in power until his death in 1953.

1934 Adolf Hitler is granted full government power, establishing a fascist dictatorship in Germany.

1936 Dictator Francisco Franco overthrows Spain's monarchy; he will remain in power until 1975.

1945 Hitler commits suicide, and Mussolini is executed, bringing an end to fascism in Germany and Italy.

1948 Juan Perón becomes dictator of Argentina.

1955 A military coup ends Perón's rule, although he will again take power from 1973 to 1974.

1966 Cameroon becomes a one-party state.

1973 Dictator Augusto Pinochet, backed by the U.S., overthrows Chilean president Salvador Allende.

1975 Pol Pot begins a brutal three-year dictatorship in Cambodia, killing as many as 2 million Cambodians.

1979 Saddam Hussein becomes president of Iraq, setting up the one-party Ba'ath government.

1988 Pinochet loses a plebiscite, a special election he initiated to extend the term of his power. The 1989 election of Patricio Aylwin restored democracy to Chile.

1990 Democratic reforms are allowed in Cameroon, but the country remains a police state.

2002 Former Serbian president Slobodan Milosevic stands trial for war crimes.

2003 The dictatorship of Iraq's Saddam Hussein is toppled by the U.S. and international allies.

Selected Bibliography

Central Intelligence Agency. *The World Factbook 2006*.
   http://www.cia.gov/cia/publications/factbook.

Fernandez-Armesto, Felipe. *Ideas That Changed the World*.
   New York: Dorling Kindersley, 2003.

Krieger, Joel, ed. *The Oxford Companion to Politics of the
   World*. New York: Oxford University Press, 1993.

Lewis, James R., and Carl Skutsch, eds. *The Human Rights
   Encyclopedia*. Armonk, N.Y.: Sharpe Reference, 2001.

Pious, Richard M. *Governments of the World*. 3 vols. New York:
   Oxford University Press, 1998.

Glossary

censorship   the practice of banning or removing controversial parts of books, newspapers, or television broadcasts

centralized   located the government in a specific place, often in a capital city, to make decisions for the whole country

communism   a system of government that discourages private ownership of property and enterprise; instead, the government manages property and enterprise on behalf of its citizens

conservatives people who are against rapid or extreme change; in the case of the Roman government, conservatives feared change would cause them to lose their wealth

constitution the basic ideas by which a country is governed, particularly as they relate to the powers of government and the rights of citizens

constitutional monarchy a form of monarchy in which the monarch serves as a government figurehead, while the true power rests in the hands of elected officials

democracies governments based on citizen participation; in most democracies, citizens vote for officials to represent their interests

depression a period of economic difficulty marked by unemployment, high prices, and low wages

dissent disagreement with accepted policies, especially regarding governments; those who disagree are called dissidents

economy the production and distribution of wealth; countries with strong economies often have wealthier citizens than those with weak economies

ethnic relating to people who share a common culture, background, or race; even if people come from the same country, they may have different ethnic backgrounds

executive	relating to the branch of government concerned with making sure laws are carried out and obeyed
genocide	the mass killing of groups of people, often because of their ethnic background or religious beliefs
human rights	rights believed to belong universally to every person, such as the right to live and to speak freely without fear of detention or torture from a government
ideological	based on a specific belief, or ideology, that serves as the foundation for specific actions or ways of thinking
legislative	relating to the lawmaking powers of government; in many countries, a parliament is the legislature, or lawmaking body
monarchy	a government in which the power is held by one person who rules for life and who has inherited the position from his or her parent
nationalism	a strong belief in the superiority and ability of a nation; national pride can be used to unify some people and exclude others
parliament	a group of officials elected to make laws in a country; many countries in Europe have a parliament

propaganda   organized publicity in the form of posters, pictures, books, and television broadcasts to arouse feelings in people, such as admiration for or fear of a political figure

regime   a specific system of government under one person; each dictator sets up his own regime according to his personality and style of government

republic   a form of government in which government officials represent citizens; republics are often, but not always, democratic

socialist   relating to a system of government based on government-run enterprise; communism goes one step beyond socialism, as its goal is to progress to public ownership of enterprise and all aspects of government

unanimous   having the consent of everyone; with all members in complete agreement

Index